TCHAIKOVSKY

Three Solos for Violin and Piano
from SWAN LAKE

Edited by Endre Granat

PIANO

Contents

KEISER®

PROGRAM NOTE

Three Solos for Violin and Piano
from SWAN LAKE

Concertmaster solos in Tchaikovsky's music take a prominent place. His third and fourth Suite (*Mozartiana*) and the second movement of the *Piano Concerto No.2* feature the solo violin. In the Imperial Ballet in St. Petersburg, the violin solos were performed by the Solo Violinist of the Tsar, a title bestowed by the tsar upon the finest violinists in all of Russia.

As the ballet solos were performed by the likes of Henri Wieniawski and Leopold Auer, the composers gave free reign to their creative inspiration and wrote some of their most gorgeous lyrical and virtuoso music for solo violin. *The White Swan Pas De Deux* and the *Black Swan Pas De Deux* are of extraordinary beauty expressing love and impending drama. The *Russian Dance* is a virtuoso showpiece foreshadowing the last movement of the composer's violin concerto.

Endre Granat, Editor

WHITE SWAN PAS DE DEUX
from the ballet *Swan Lake*

Edited by
ENDRE GRANAT

PETER ILYICH TCHAIKOVSKY
Op. 20

Andante non troppo

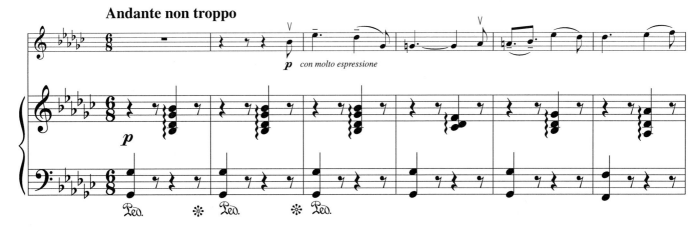

8

Tempo I

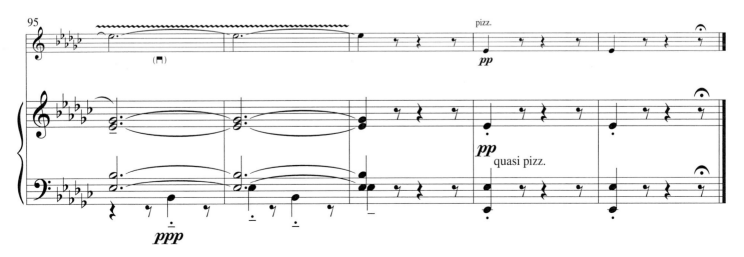

BLACK SWAN PAS DE DEUX

from the ballet *Swan Lake*

Edited by
ENDRE GRANAT

PETER ILYICH TCHAIKOVSKY
Op. 20

WHITE SWAN PAS DE DEUX
from the ballet *Swan Lake*

Edited by
ENDRE GRANAT

PETER ILYICH TCHAIKOVSKY
Op. 20

Violin

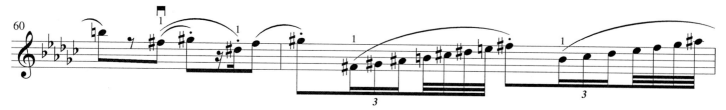

Violin

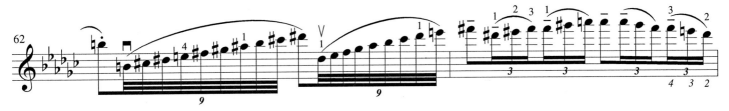

Tempo I

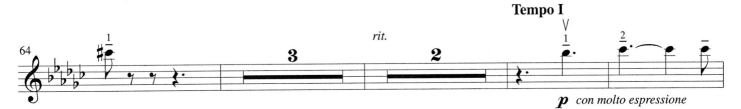

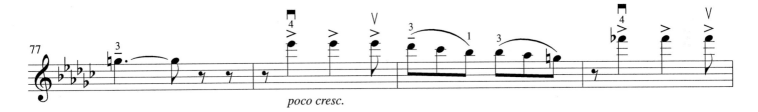

BLACK SWAN PAS DE DEUX
from the ballet *Swan Lake*

Edited by
ENDRE GRANAT

PETER ILYICH TCHAIKOVSKY
Op. 20

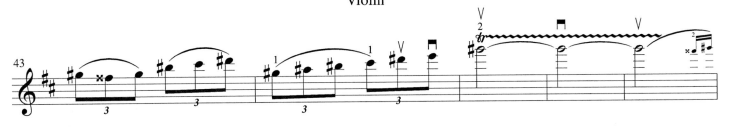

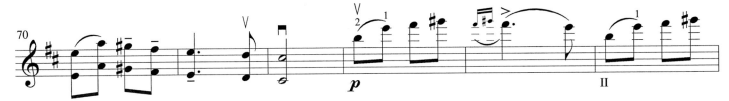

RUSSIAN DANCE
from the ballet *Swan Lake*

Edited by
ENDRE GRANAT

PETER ILYICH TCHAIKOVSKY
Op. 20

Violin

8

Violin

PROGRAM NOTE

Three Solos for Violin and Piano
from SWAN LAKE

Concertmaster solos in Tchaikovsky's music take a prominent place. His third and fourth Suite (*Mozartiana*) and the second movement of the *Piano Concerto No.2* feature the solo violin. In the Imperial Ballet in St. Petersburg, the violin solos were performed by the Solo Violinist of the Tsar, a title bestowed by the tsar upon the finest violinists in all of Russia.

As the ballet solos were performed by the likes of Henri Wieniawski and Leopold Auer, the composers gave free reign to their creative inspiration and wrote some of their most gorgeous lyrical and virtuoso music for solo violin. *The White Swan Pas De Deux* and the *Black Swan Pas De Deux* are of extraordinary beauty expressing love and impending drama. The *Russian Dance* is a virtuoso showpiece foreshadowing the last movement of the composer's violin concerto.

Endre Granat, Editor

Violin

About the Editor

Endre Granat has studied with Zoltan Kodaly, Gyorgy Ligeti and Jascha Heifetz and is the premier concertmaster for the Hollywood film industry. He has performed with legendary conductors George Szell, Sir Georg Solti and Zubin Mehta. He is a Laureate of the Queen Elizabeth International competition and recipient of the Grand Prix du Disque and the Ysaye Medal.

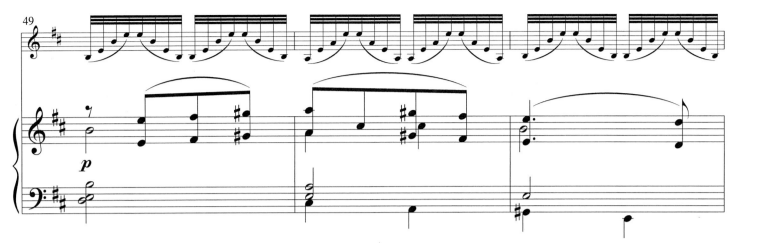

RUSSIAN DANCE
from the ballet *Swan Lake*

Edited by
ENDRE GRANAT

PETER ILYICH TCHAIKOVSKY
Op. 20

Cadenza

Andante semplice

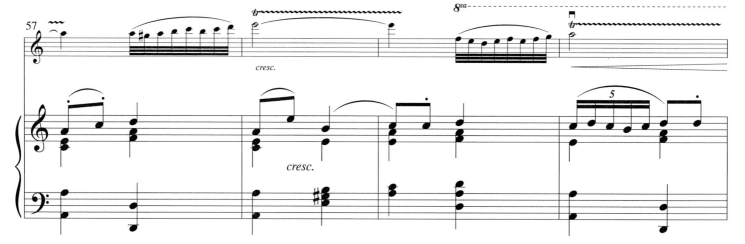

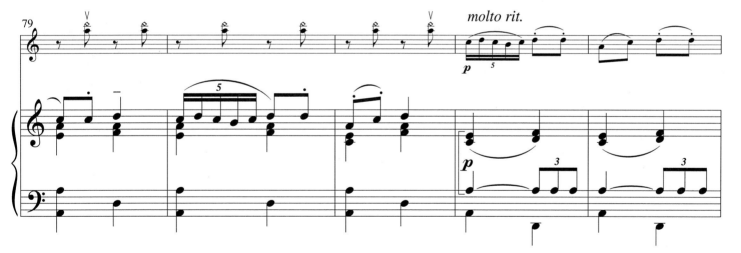

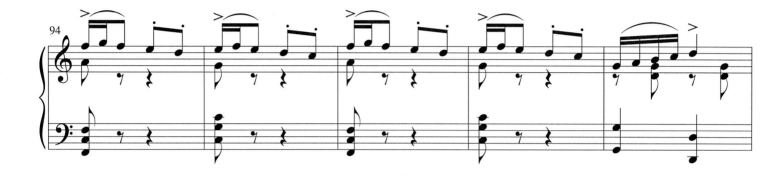

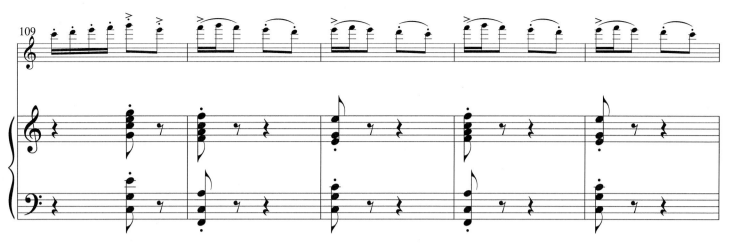

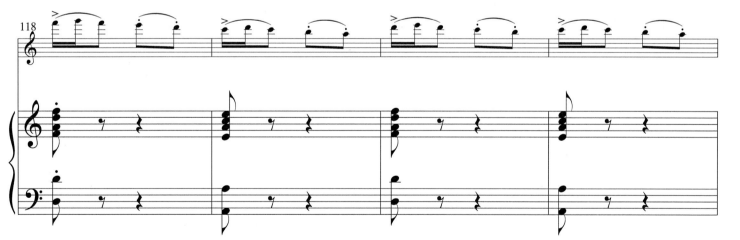

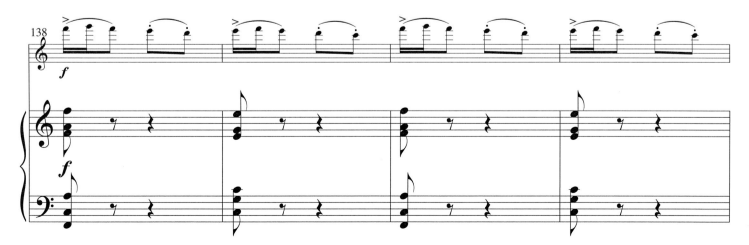

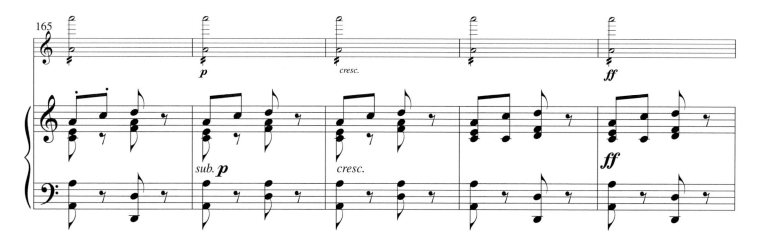